W9-AFX-174

GOFF-NELSON MEMORIAL LIBRARY
41 Lake Street
Tupper Lake, New York 12986

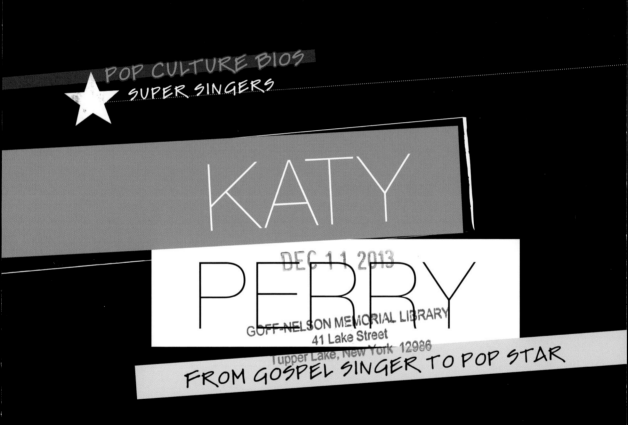

POP CULTURE BIOS

SUPER SINGERS

KATY

PERRY

FROM GOSPEL SINGER TO POP STAR

NADIA HIGGINS

DEC 11 2013

GOFF-NELSON MEMORIAL LIBRARY
41 Lake Street
Tupper Lake, New York 12986

Lerner Publications Company

MINNEAPOLIS

Copyright © 2013 by Lerner Publishing Group, Inc.

All rights reserved. International copyright secured. No part of
this book may be reproduced, stored in a retrieval system, or
transmitted in any form or by any means—electronic, mechanical,
photocopying, recording, or otherwise—without the prior written
permission of Lerner Publishing Group, Inc., except for the
inclusion of brief quotations in an acknowledged review.

Lerner Publications Company
A division of Lerner Publishing Group, Inc.
241 First Avenue North
Minneapolis, MN 55401 U.S.A.

Website address: www.lernerbooks.com

Library of Congress Cataloging-in-Publication Data

Higgins, Nadia.
     Katy Perry : from gospel singer to pop star / by Nadia
Higgins.
          p.   cm. — (Pop culture bios: super singers)
     Includes bibliographical references and index.
     ISBN 978-0-7613-4145-1 (lib. bdg. : alk. paper)
     1. Perry, Katy—Juvenile literature. 2. Singers—United
States—Biography—Juvenile literature. I. Title.
ML3930.P455H54 2013
782.42164092—dc23 [B]   2012004577

Manufactured in the United States of America
1 – PP – 7/15/12

INTRODUCTION

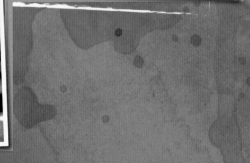

"**I** am a girl. I am allowed to be emotional."

Katy Perry is practically glowing in a shimmery white minidress. On the front, a bubble gum machine spills polka dots down the skirt. It's November 2010, and Katy owns the stage as she performs at the BBC Radio 1 Teen Awards in London, England. Next up is her favorite song, "Firework."

"Thank you for supporting this song so much," Katy goes on. "Because it means the world to me." Her voice cracks on the word *world*, and her blue-green eyes are suddenly filled with tears.

But when the beat starts pounding, Katy's on again. She pumps a fist in the air. Then her whole body's bouncing. The crowd is a sea of waving arms by the time she breaks into the chorus. Her fans—her Katycats—are singing their hearts out.

Katy has said that "Firework" is about how everybody holds a spark of greatness. As with all of her songs, "Firework"

CHORUS =
the part of a song
that repeats

6

comes from her own life. And there's no doubt that Katy's own spark has exploded into fireworks.

As the song ends, Katy's up on the shoulders of two dancers. She's got both arms straight overhead. The crowd is going crazy! This is Katy's party, and she's loving every second.

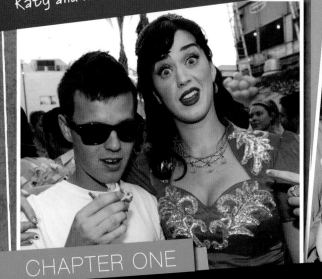

Katy and her brother, David, in 2008

Katy and her sister, Angela, in 2008

CHAPTER ONE

CHRISTIAN ROOTS

Katy with her parents in 2010

Funny, funky, and undoubtedly adorbs, Katy Perry is sometimes known as the class clown of pop. She's also famous for being edgy, naughty, and groundbreaking in both music and fashion. Her friends say she's hardworking and oh-so determined. One thing's for sure. Katy follows her own rules—with a wink and a cartwheel.

And just look where that has taken her. The sassy star has burned up the charts in more than twenty-five countries. She's won tons of awards and sold millions of albums. In 2011, she became the first female artist ever to have six Top 40 hits at the same time.

TOP 40 =
the most popular forty songs in the United States in a given week

Pastors' Daughter

Katy Perry is full of surprises. And one of them is her past. She was born Katheryn Elizabeth Hudson on October 25, 1984, in Santa Barbara, California. She grew up as the middle child of three in a strict Christian home. Both her parents are pastors.

Katy's parents wanted to protect her from what they felt were negative influences. So they played only gospel music at home. The only book they had around was the Bible, and most TV shows and movies were off-limits. On Halloween, the family turned off the lights and stayed in. Katy's parents thought it was wrong to celebrate a holiday that's all about ghosts, goblins, and other dark creatures.

For several years, Katy's family lived all around the United States. Her parents preached wherever they were welcome. Katy got used to changing schools and making new friends. She got used to times when money was tight.

LUCKY SHE'S BLESSED

Katy wasn't allowed to use the word *lucky* when she was growing up. It sounded too much like *Lucifer*, a name for the devil. To this day, Katy uses the word *blessed* instead.

GOSPEL =
an emotional style of
Christian music

OUCH!

Katy's family couldn't afford to take Katy to the dentist for several years. When she finally did go, she had thirteen cavities!

A Spunky Kid

Katy was a happy, active kid. Her legs were covered in bruises from climbing trees and jumping off stuff. She loved to surf and skateboard. When she was eight, her dad started bringing her to garage sales. Katy had a knack for finding cool, old treasures. Her unique style was already showing.

At nine, Katy started singing in church. Her parents saw that she had talent. They signed her up for singing lessons and then guitar lessons. Katy's father began paying her $10 every time she sang for people—whether it was at church groups, birthday parties, family gatherings, or wherever! Katy loved to work a crowd.

A "Magical Moment"

Katy had always gone to Christian schools. But in ninth grade, she started attending a public school near Santa Barbara. Her friends introduced her to pop music. Whenever she went to the home of a friend who had cable TV, the first thing she'd do was turn on MTV.

Katy's ninth-grade school picture

She started to sneak pop music home. She'd listen with headphones *and* under a blanket so her parents wouldn't hear.

At a sleepover, Katy heard the '70s rock band Queen. "You know how everyone has their own magical moment in hearing something they love?" Katy asked in an interview with *Esquire* magazine. **"That happened to me with Queen."**

Katy was inspired by glam rocker Freddie Mercury. Here he performs with Queen in 1985.

From that instant on, Katy was gaga for Freddie Mercury, Queen's lead singer. He was a glam rocker and way over-the-top in everything from his attitude to his music. Things were shaking up in Katy's world.

Christian Singer

Meanwhile, Katy was still singing at church. One day, a talent scout from the Christian music industry spotted her. He saw a star in the making.

Katy was thrilled that the scout liked her singing! She started dreaming of

TALENT SCOUT =
a person who finds unknown
artists and helps them to
build a career

making it big. Her parents encouraged her to go for her dreams. At fourteen, Katy began spending lots of time in Nashville, Tennessee, the heart of the Christian music scene. She made lots of friends in the city. She'd spend weeks at a time in Nashville, crashing on friends' floors or lumpy couches. She started writing and recording Christian songs. She played the guitar so much her fingers hurt.

At fifteen, Katy dropped out of school to focus full-time on her music. Soon she signed on with a Christian recording company and cut her first album, *Katy Hudson*. It's a far cry from what Katycats know today. At this point, Katy's "teenage dream" seemed more prayer than party.

Katy's album didn't even sell two hundred copies before the company tanked. Katy was sixteen and had no clue what she should do next.

HIGH SCHOOL: TAKE 2

After Katy left high school, she kept on studying on her own. She went on to pass her GED test, an exam that lets people earn a high school degree without attending classes.

CHAPTER TWO

THE NEW KATY

Katy rocks her new look after turning from Christian music to pop.

GOFF-NELSON MEMORIAL LIBRARY
41 Lake Street
Tupper Lake, New York 12986

By seventeen, Katy had started over. She was now Katy Perry, not Katy Hudson. (Perry had been her mom's last name before she'd married. Katy took the name so people wouldn't confuse her with the actress Kate Hudson.) She was done with Christian music. She was living in Los Angeles trying to make it in the world of pop.

Why did Katy change? Some people say she turned her back on her Christian roots so she could get famous. But Katy says no way. She just felt that her world had opened up. **"I've gone from living in a 1-D world to a 3-D world,"** she dished to *InStyle* magazine when asked about her transformation. She explained that she was psyched to explore everything she'd missed as a kid.

HER JESUS TATTOO

Katy has *Jesus* tattooed in loopy cursive on her wrist. She got the tattoo when she was eighteen. It was to always remind her where she came from. To this day, Katy considers herself a Christian.

Tough Times

Katy knew she needed an ally in Los Angeles—someone to help her get ahead. One day she was watching VH1 and saw an interview with big-time producer Glen Ballard. He had helped one of Katy's all-time favorite singers, Alanis Morissette, make it to the top. Katy set up an audition with the music guru. She wowed him right away! He agreed to help her get a recording deal ASAP.

PRODUCER =
a music professional who helps musicians record their best album possible

In 2003, Katy signed with a major recording label. She spent a year working on an album—until the bosses changed their minds. Katy was dropped.

Then, in 2004, Katy got a second break. She signed with another major recording company. She almost finished another album when (again!) the label dropped her. The head honchos thought she wouldn't stand out!

It took a while for Katy to climb to the heights she knows today.

Did Katy have what it took to survive in the pop music biz? Did she have both the talent *and* the confidence? She wasn't sure anymore. Later, she would tell *Billboard* magazine how helpless she felt. "I used to just feel numb," she spilled. "It was like taking a kid to Disneyland and making them wait outside. The people just wouldn't let me through the gates."

Plus, Katy was broke. She scraped by doing whatever work she could find. One position she took was an office job for a music company. She sat at a desk all day and listened to demos by other artists. It was up to her to spot the next big star—when all she wanted was to be a big star herself! For Katy, it was pretty sucktastic.

DEMO =
a sample of music an artist puts together to show to recording companies

LISTEN UP, KATYCATS!

What advice would Katy give to someone who wants to follow in her footsteps?

1. Learn to play a musical instrument.
2. Perform every chance you get—at cafés, restaurants, churches, and anywhere else they'll give you a stage!
3. Don't take no for an answer.

Finally!

Would anybody want Katy after she'd been dropped two times? In late 2006, an answer came from Capitol Records—yes! The top dogs here were not only smitten with Katy's style and sound. They also knew how tough she was. They knew she could handle the pressures of fame.

Katy had written about seventy songs by then. Some of them were good enough for a new album. Still, Katy needed a smash hit. Capitol brought in top songwriters to work with her.

Katy says the chorus for "I Kissed a Girl" popped into her head one morning in the shower. In May 2008, the catchy single stormed the world of pop music. Everybody was talking about Katy. And some people were not happy.

SINGLE = a song that is sold by itself, not as part of an album

They said the song was immoral because it encouraged teens to be gay. Others said it was disrespectful *to* gay people. They said Katy was just pretending to be gay to sell her music.

To Katy, it was just a fun song about a girl crush she'd really had. She told the British *Observer,* **"I play music. I'm not running for president. If only the world would stop walking on eggshells and get a sense of humor."**

KITTY PURRY

Katy luvs her cat, Kitty Purry. So why wasn't she psyched to hug Kitty during the video for "I Kissed a Girl"? It's 'cuz she's freaked out by cat hair! She absolutely *hates* getting it on her clothes. She felt like running for a lint roller every five seconds.

CHAPTER THREE

CLASS CLOWN OF POP

Katy's album *One of the Boys* became the summer smash of 2008. Her life became a blur of travel from one publicity event to the next. She could hardly walk down the street or eat at a restaurant without a fan coming up to her. Did Katy complain? No way! She tried every day to stay grateful for her amazing success.

PUBLICITY EVENT =
an event, such as a TV interview, meant to spread the word about an artist

Fruit + Cats + Katycats

Meanwhile, Katy started getting ready for her first world tour. Her number one goal for the Hello Katy show? Fun! So she themed the show around two of her favorite things—fruit and cats. Random? Maybe. Playful? Totes! That's Katy Perry.

The tour ran for most of 2009. During each show, Katy changed from one cat suit to the next. She bounced giant blow-up strawberries across the arena like beach balls.

Giant blow-up strawberries were a big part of the Hello Katy tour.

Snack: kettle corn (sweet-and-salty popcorn)

Fruit: pineapple

Junk food: Chicken McNuggets

Can't-live-without item: silk sleep mask

Way to exercise: jumping rope (She does it before every show.)

Way to relax: cleaning her house (She's a neat freak.)

BFFs: designer Markus Molinari (RIGHT, WITH KATY) and singer Rihanna

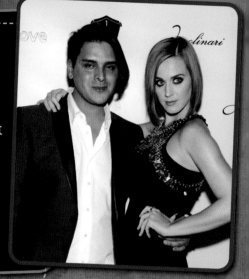

Her Teenage Dream

By the fall of 2009, something else exciting was happening in Katy's life. She had met British comedian Russell Brand the year before at the filming of a comedy movie. Russell was starring in the movie, and Katy played a minor role (which was later cut). She ran into Russell again at a rehearsal for an awards show in New York City. She jokingly threw an empty water bottle at his head to get his attention. It totally worked! The pair began dating shortly after. They got engaged that New Year's Eve while riding on an elephant in India.

REHEARSAL = a practice run of a live show

As always, Katy poured her feelings into her music. She wrote "Teenage Dream" and "E.T." about her cloud-nine feelings for Russell. That winter and spring, she worked hard on her next album, *Teenage Dream*. In a way, the stakes were even higher this time. Katy had to surprise fans with a new sound. At the same time, she couldn't disappoint them by going too far off track. Katy's answer? Get dancier. Katy made sure this album would get people sweaty!

Katy and Russell Brand

Branching Out

Meanwhile, Katy seemed even busier. As a guest judge on *American Idol*, Katy showed—once again—that she was a gal who spoke her mind. She didn't hesitate to give performers the real scoop on what she thought of their singing. Then, when her *American Idol* gig was up, she turned on her sweet side to perform the voice of Smurfette for *The Smurfs* movie.

Katy shows off her sparkly Smurfette dress while promoting *The Smurfs* movie.

As the summer of 2010 wound down, Katy was getting ready to launch her own perfume, Purr. This floral and fruity scent would be sold in purple cat-shaped bottles. Katy couldn't wait to introduce the fragrance to her fans!

Teenage Dream also came out around this time. But Katy soon found herself in the news for another reason. A skit she'd done for *Sesame Street* was being pulled at the last minute. Parents thought the green dress she wore during the video was too low-cut for preschoolers.

THANKS, KATY!

Another reason to be friends with Katy? She wears most of her adorable outfits just one time. Then she gives them away to friends.

Married Life

In October 2010, Katy and Russell were married in India. But rumors about the couple started swirling right away. Magazines and websites claimed that Russell was cheating—or that Katy was cheating. They said the pair's romance was on the rocks. The rumors made Katy stabby—so she stopped reading them. Her 2011 New Year's resolution? No more Googling herself!

COME ON OVER!

Katy and Russell moved into a cool old house in Los Angeles. They put a huge tepee on the front lawn. They filled it with pillows so their friends could come over and hang out on warm evenings.

Katy and Russell shortly after their wedding

It takes a couple of hours to do Katy's makeup for a show. All the prep makes Katy impatient! So instead of just sitting there while her makeup artists work their magic, Katy catches a few z's. She even ordered a comfy dentist's chair that she can lie back in while she gets glammed. When she wakes up, she looks fab!

In February 2011, Katy began her yearlong California Dreams tour. This time, Katy's theme was candy. She oversaw every detail to make sure the show was epic. The tour featured piped-in candy smells, a cotton-candy cloud, a candy-cane staircase, dancing gingerbread men, and no fewer than twenty outfit changes for Katy!

Katy made sure to have at least one night with Russell for every two nights on the stage. But somewhere along the way, things fell apart. In December 2011, Russell filed for divorce.

Change Ahead

Katy has been super private about the breakup. But in January 2012, she tweeted, "I am so grateful for all the love and support I've had from people around the world. You guys have made my heart happy again." Katy's next plans are just to keep on growing as a person so she can write more awesome songs. She revealed to interviewer Barbara Walters that **"I hope to be changing to the last day I'm on this Earth."** If Katy's ever-evolving, ever-exciting past is any indication, she'll have no trouble meeting that goal!

KATY
PICS!

SOURCE NOTES

5   *Katy Perry—Teenage Dream and Firework—BBC Radio Teen Awards HD,* YouTube video, 9:14, posted by MrJpeguxo, December 4, 2010, http://www.youtube.com/watch?feature =player_embedded&v=MW133yJNNnA#! (January 30, 2012).

5   Ibid.

12   David Curcurito, "And She Can Sing: An Esquire Investigation into Katy Perry," *Esquire,* April 2009, http://galegroup.com (December 23, 2011).

15   Lizzie Widdicombe, "A Different Shade of Katy," *InStyle,* October 2011, http://www .ebscohost.com (December 23, 2011).

17   Monica Herrera, "Katy Perry: Girlie Action," *Billboard,* July 31, 2010, http://www.ebscohost .com (December 23, 2011).

19   *Gale Biography in Context,* s.v. "Katy Perry," http://ic.galegroup.com (December 23, 2011).

27   Katy Perry, Twitter, posted on January 7, 2012.

27   "Barbara Walters' 2011 Fascinating People: Katy Perry Interview," YouTube video, 4:07, posted by KatyPerryLicious, December 14, 2011, http://www.youtube.com/watch?v =Xjt75_8jjVE (January 30, 2012).

MORE KATY INFO

BOP & Tiger Beat Online: Katy Perry
http://www.bopandtigerbeat.com/tag/katy-perry
Find awesome updates for Katycats from this reliable celeb mag. While you're there, vote on your favorite Katy hairdos and dresses.

Johnson, Robin. *Katy Perry.* New York: Crabtree Publishing Company, 2012.
Learn more about Katy's childhood, her music, and her rise to fame.

Kaplan, Arie. *American Pop Music: Hit Makers, Superstars, and Dance Revolutionaries.* Minneapolis: Twenty-First Century Books, 2013.
Pop music fans will find lots to love in this in-depth look at American pop.

Katy Perry
http://www.katyperry.com
Check out Katy's official site to find tour dates, download ringtones, and connect with other Katycats. You can also buy a cute blue wig!

Katy's Facebook Page
http://www.facebook.com/katyperry
Visit Katy's FB page to learn all the latest Katy news.

Landau, Elaine. *Beyoncé: R & B Superstar.* Minneapolis: Lerner Publications Company, 2013.
Like reading about Katy Perry? Then you'll love reading about Beyoncé, another of the music world's most amazing talents.

INDEX

The images in this book are used with the permission of: © Jason LeVeris/FilmMagic/Getty Images, pp. 2, 27; © Albert L. Ortega/WireImage/Getty Images, pp. 3 (top), 14 (bottom); © Kevin Nixon/Future Publishing via Getty Images, p. 3 (bottom), 20 (bottom right); © Kevin Mazur/WireImage for The CW Network/Getty Images, p. 4 (top); © Reuters/David McNew/Landov, p. 4 (middle); John Angelillo/UPI/Landov, p. 4 (bottom); Zuma Press/Newscom, pp. 5, 6, 7 © Jesse Grant/Getty Images For EMI Music, p. 8 (top left); © Florian Seefried/Getty Images, p. 8 (top right); © Jeff Kravitz/Film Magic/Getty Images, p. 8 (bottom); Seth Poppel Yearbook Library, p. 11; © Dave Hogan/Hulton Archives/Getty Images, p. 13; © Amy Graves/WireImage/Getty Images, p. 14 (top); David McNew/Reuters/Landov, p. 15; © Mike Guastella/WireImage/Getty Images, p. 16; © Noel Vasquez/Getty Images, p. 18; © Peter Brooker/Rex Features/Presselect/Alamy, p. 19; RHA/ZOB WENN Photos/Newscom, p. 20 (top); © Jon Kopaloff/FilmMagic/Getty Images, p. 20 (bottom left); © Brian Sweeney/Getty Images, p. 21; © David Becker/WireImage/Getty Images, p. 22; Hubert Boesl/dpa/Landov, p. 23 (top); © Jason LeVeris/FilmMagic/Newscom, p. 23 (bottom); © George Pimentel/WireImage/Getty Images, p. 24; © Dave J Hogan/Stringer/Getty Images, p. 25; Stuart Castle/WENN Photos/Newscom, p. 26; © Jason LeVeris/FilmMagic/Getty Images, p. 27; © s_bukley/Shutterstock.com, pp. 28 (top left), 28 (bottom left); Mario Anzuoni/Reuters/Landov, p. 28 (right); © Anton Oparin/Shutterstock.com, p. 29 (top right); © Carrienelson1/Dreamstime.com, p. 29 (top middle); © Helga Esteb/Shutterstock.com, p. 29 (right); © Kristian Dowling/Getty Images, p. 29 (bottom).

Front cover: © Jason LaVeris/FilmMagic/Getty Images (right); © Kevin Winter/AMA2010/Getty Images for DCP (left); back cover: © s_bukley/Shutterstock.com.

Main body text set in Shannon Std Book 12/18.
Typeface provided by Monotype Typography.

DEC 1

GOFF-NELSON MEMORIAL LIBRARY
41 Lake Street
Tupper Lake, New York 12986